AWAY   FROM   KEYBOARD

WHY DON'T YOU JUST SWITCH OFF YOUR WIFI AND
GO AND DO SOMETHING LESS BORING INSTEAD?

ANNA-MARIA KIOSSE & CALLUM SHOVE

Please stick your
photograph here:

WELCOME

Yeah, yeah,yeah... We get it. Computer
games are educational.The internet sets
you free.Your phone makes you sociable.
Digital experiences can make you smarter,
faster and more dexterous.
We should integrate digital technology
into every aspect of our lives.
Internet of things. Blah blah blaaaah...

NOBODY IS, DISPUTING THAT DIGITAL IS COOL.

But tell me, isnt it time you created something
with your own hands?

Go on.
Come back into the real world.

(this text was written on an oldschool thing.
A typewriter. Yeah! Cool huh? Not a computer.)

imagination is More →IMPORTANT← than knowledge!

WHICH IS GOOD BECAUSE THERE IS ALWAYS FAR TOO MUCH KNOWLEDGE TO KNOW.

WHEREAS YOU ALREADY HAVE ALL THE IMAGINATION YOU WILL EVER NEED.
AFK IS A SECRET MISSION, NOBODY KNOWS ABOUT IT. WELL, OBVIOUSLY I JUST TOLD YOU — BUT NOBODY ELSE APART FROM THAT. SO ANYWAY, THE IDEA IS TO UNLOCK THE AWESOME POWERS OF YOUR IMAGINATION.

WE CAN PROUDLY GUARANTEE THAT THERE WILL BE ABSOLUTELY NO KNOWLEDGE INSIDE THIS BOOK!!!!

GOOD LUCK GRASSHOPPER! REMEMBER — THIS IS SUPPOSED TO BE FUN!

THIS BOOK BELONGS TO:

NAME: _____

AGE: _____

SECRET WEAPON: _____

SUPER POWER: _____

PARTNER IN CRIME: _____

FAVOURITE COLOUR: _____

In case of loss
please return to _____

REWARD: _____

HOw to use

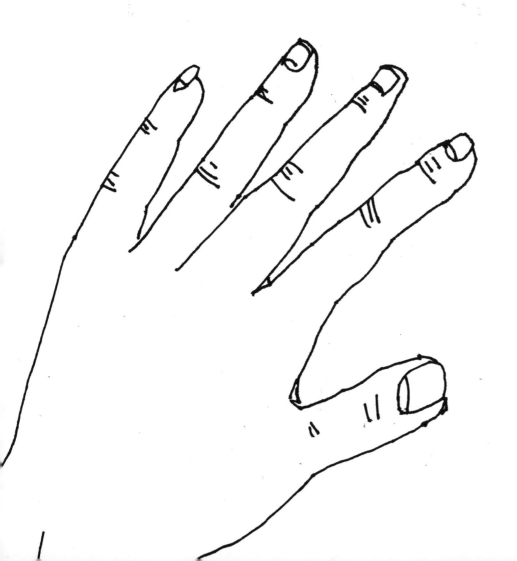

this book:

AFK is a highly interactive book for expanding creative minds (that's you()). Packed with hundreds of questions, missions and random challenges - just grab it, flick it open and play.

Every page throws up different possibilities. Sometimes they are questions provoking thought & encouraging creative writing or drawing. Sometimes they are mini - creative challenges. Sometimes they are just for laughs.

Get around the problem of the blank page, 'I don't know what to draw.' or 'I don't know what to write about.' AFK is here to get you started.

Remember: This is not homework.

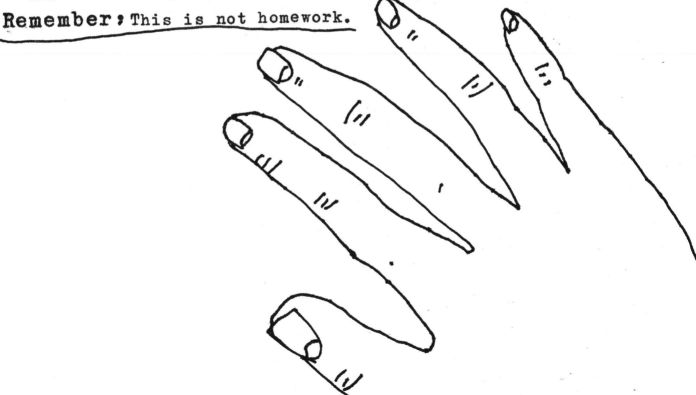

AFK ONCE A DAY KEEPS BOREDOM AT BAY!!

-traditional saying

GO ON SWITCH OFF THE SCREEN
LOG OUT.
SHUT DOWN.
POWER OFF.

....AND GO AND DO STUFF!

BELIEVE.

EVERYTHING IS NOT BORING.

YOU WILL NOT BE BORED.

GO AFK TODAY!

YOU. MUST. CREATE.

*HEYA!

WARNING!
These tasks are not homework.
You can do them any way you
like. you can change them.
You can ignore them. You can just
eat the page.* You can persuade an
animal to do them for you. you
can send them to a friend. You can
soak them in vinegar and slap yourself
around the face with them.
Or you could just DO THEM.
JUST DO THEM.

*dont eat the page it's got loads of weird
chemicals, including bumbagridiumthermalpantsaryde.

in it

SUPER
INK!

ARE YOU READY TO RUMBLE?!

GET YOUR TEAM TOGETHER!

- [x] THE AFK BOOK
- [ ] COLOURED PENCILS
- [ ] MARKERS
- [ ] SCISSORS
- [ ] GLUE STICK
- [ ] FANTASY & IMAGINATION
- [ ] GOOD MOOD

CHAPTER
ONE

ALL ABOUT ME

Hey you!

hey buddy

w

HEY GUY!

do you think you are? HEY RELAX. the what now
Did I come on too strong? Just who in the what now

YOU ARE THE GUY.

I LOVE YOU.
Yeah I said it. Now are you gonna answer
these questions or WHAT?
I love you. Ah I'm just a book...
What do I know...?

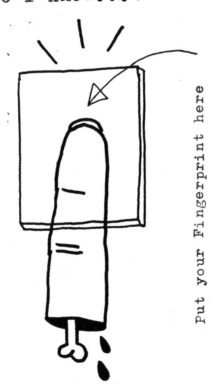

Put your Fingerprint here

My Nickname:

My best friend:

The coolest thing in the world:

My favorite food:

Things I collect:

My dream car:

Famous people who have
the same name as me:

If I was to win a gold medal at the Olympics it would
likely be for:

 My dream job:

If I could eat one thing for the rest of my life,
it would be:

My ideal packed lunch would be:

My favourite cartoon character :

My ideal pocket money amount would be:

My favourite computer game:

my favourite book:

The food items that should be banned forever:

MY 7 DAY drawing CHALLENGE

A Drawing Each day

For a whole week
You can draw whatever you
want. As long as it's cool and makes
you happy. Remember it should be
fun! It can be a sock, a bird, a
pizza, a person, an animal and it doesn't
need to be perfect. Go FOR IT!

DAY 1

DAY 2

DAY 3

DAY 5

DAY 4

DAY 6

DAY 7

EITHER/OR

You can have one and not the other
FOR THE REST OF YOUR LIFE.
You have three seconds to decide or
they will both disappear foreverand
you will never remember anything
about either of them.
MUM or DAD? No sorry ...that is a
bit harsh. Skip that one ;)

RICH or FAMOUS
SWEET or SALTED
AMUSEMENT PARK or WATER PARK
MOVIES or MUSIC
DOGS or CATS
SUMMER or WINTER
CITY or COUNTRY
SUBWAY or McDONALDS
BATMAN or SUPERMAN
HERO or VILLAIN

PIZZA or HOT DOG
APPETIZER or DESSERT
SLOW or FAST
SOUP or SALAD
BRAINS or BEAUTY
VAMPIRES or WEREWOLVES
COOKIE or CUPCAKE
BATH or SHOWER
CHOCOLATE or CHIPS
BE ABLE TO FLY or TO READ PEOPLE'S MIND

GET
Emotional
CrEAte YOUR OVn SEt OF EmOjis

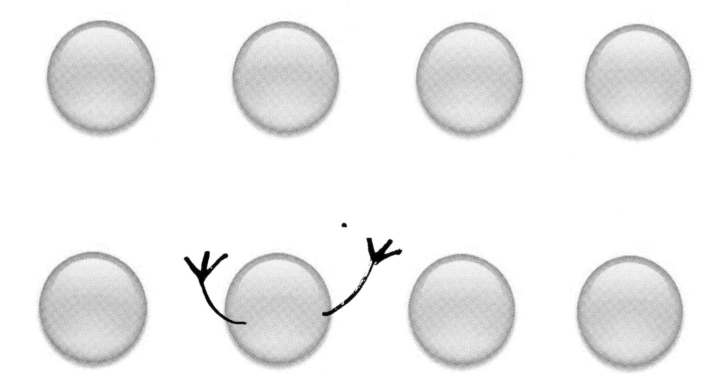

QUICKFIRE!

HAVE YOU EVER...

- ☐ WON A TROPHY
- ☐ LEARNT A FOREIGN LANGUAGE
- ☐ RIDDEN IN A LIMO
- ☐ FLOWN IN A PLANE
- ☐ MET SOMEONE FAMOUS
- ☐ BROKEN SOMETHING EXPENSIVE
- ☐ JUMPED OFF THE HIGH BOARD
- ☐ BEEN ON TV
- ☐ SENT A MESSAGE IN A BOTTLE
- ☐ CAUGHT A FISH
- ☐ GROWN A PLANT
- ☐ BROKEN A BONE
- ☐ SEEN A FOX
- ☐ EATEN WITH CHOPSTICKS
- ☐ FIRED A BOW AND ARROW
- ☐ RIDDEN A (MECHANICAL) BULL
- ☐ CHEATED IN A TEST
- ☐ CHASED A RAINBOW
- ☐ SEEN A SHOOTING STAR
- ☐ BAKED A CAKE
- ☐ SLEPT UNDER THE STARS
- ☐ DID SOMETHING FORBIDDEN
- ☐ RIDDEN A HORSE
- ☐ SEEN A GHOST
- ☐ SOLVED RUBIKS CUBE

FIND A PHOTO OF
SOMETHING THAT STARTS
WITH EACH LETTER OF
YOUR NAME: & STICK
THEM HERE:

THINK ABOUT THIS

YOU ARE A ROCKSTAR!
WHAT'S THE NAME OF YOUR BAND?

BANDNAME:
_____

YOU ARE A SUPERHERO!
WHAT'S YOUR NAME?

SUPERHERO NAME:
_____

YOU COULD BE ANYWHERE IN THE
WORLD RIGHT NOW. WHERE WOULD
YOU CHOOSE BE?

PLACE:
_____

IF YOU COULD HAVE ANY
ANIMAL AS A PET,

IT WOULD BE:
_____

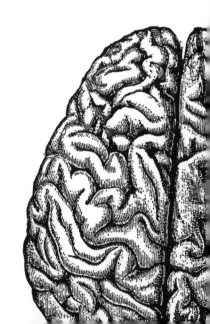

CREATE YOUR FAMILY COAT OF ARMS

Trace back your family tree far enough and you'll hit monkey. But somewhere along the road, if you're lucky, maybe you'll find an old aristocratic family connection. Probably just a whole load of smelly beggars living in muddy ditches by the road...
No matter! You can have a coat of arms anyway.
Just make up one... Here's a little help.

KING

WEIRD SYMBOL
For a good coat of arms you need a weird thing. Just whatever...

TITLE
A bold decleration of rank. Can be your name, your dogs name, or just Banana Joe...

SECRET RIVER
Well we say river it can also be a gummy worm in rainbow colours or a honey river on your toast or just a bacon strip

LEGENDARY CREATURE
As an example the famous three legged pigeon. You can use whatever you want as long as it can fly, seen before: flying horse, 5 winged pig...

MYTHICAL CREATURE
we chose the three eyed wolf, but for you it can be your pony, cat or grandmas fast chicken...

MYSTIC OBJECT
we use the mystic oracle potato. But your version can be anything, maybe your first toy or your grandads old sock.

STRONG OBJECT
An object that means a lot to you and that shows how brave you are. This can be your first trophy or your favorite spoon....

THE SHIELD
The Shield, main element and therefore the main thing in your coat of arms. Could be classic shield, a mirror, or a BBQ plate.

A POWERFUL LINE

RIBBON
A piece of material which for some reason has to have a forked cut at the end. Add your slogan, a recipe or your favorite songtitle.

>>> MAKE SURE to COLOUR IT IN! <<<

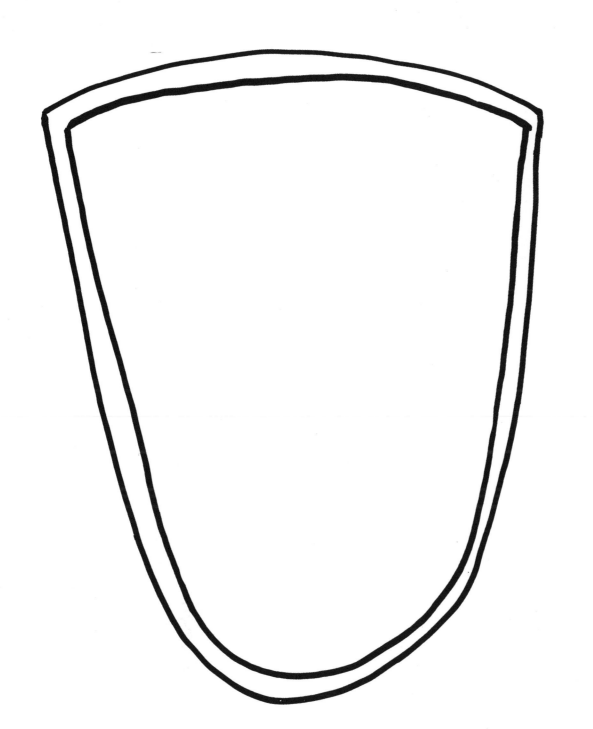

MY "BEST" FRIENDS

DRAW THE AVATARS of YOUR BEST FRIENDS!

CON-GRATS

you are

AFK for 30 PAGES

KEEP GOING FOR MORE ADVENTURES

50 THINGS I ABSOLUTELY LOVE

1.
2.
3.
4.
5.
6.
7.
8.
9.
10.
11.
12.
13.
14.
15.

16.
17.
18.
19.
20.
21.
22.
23.
24.
25.
26.
27.
28.
29.
30.

31.
32.
33.
34.
35.
36.
37.
38.
39.
40.
41.
42.
43.

44.
45.
46.
47.
48.
49.
50.

TIME TO MEASURE SOME THINGS

How high can you jump? _____

How far can you jump? _____

How long is your hair? _____

How tall are you right   at   this moment?
_____

How tall are you 3 hours later? _____

How long is your left arm? _____

How long is your right leg? _____

How tall are your mum and dad? _____

How long is your nose? _____

How long is the pen you're filling this out with?

and two more! You choose!

How long is...... '

How far ....

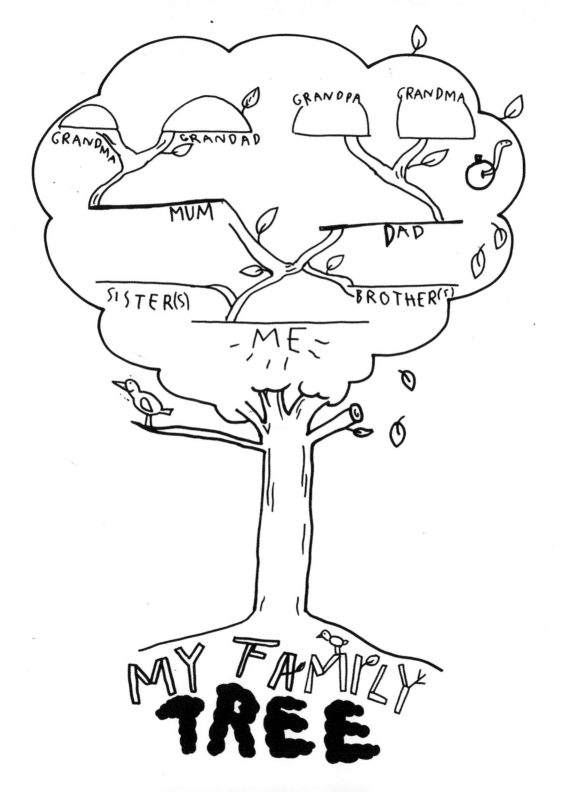

WHEN WAS THE LAST TIME YOU DID SOMETHING FOR THE FIRST TIME?

MY FIRST FRIEND:

_____

My first SCHOOL:

MY FIRST TEACHER:
___

MY FIRST holiday:

MY FIRST WOUND!

MY FIRST PET
___

my first BOOK:
___

MY FIRST HERO:
___

DRAW YOUR BREAKFAST*

*IF IT IS A PILE OF PASTA REMEMBER: START WITH ONE SPAGHETTI

ON THE SPECIAL PLATE!

MY TOP 5

BOOKS

1. AFK
2.
3.
4.
5.

MOVIES

1.
2.
3.
4.
5.

PLACES

1.
2.
3.
4.
5.

CARTOONS

1.
2.
3.
4.
5.

FONTS ARE FUN

YOU CAN
USE SHADOWS!

...OR
CURVY LINES...

...OR
SLIME...

...OR
FILL THE
LETTERS...

...OR USE
SIMPLE THIN
LINES...

...YOUR "O" CAN
BE ANYTHING...

...SOME LETTERS
CAN BE ANIMALS...

Now its on you. Create your very own & very special

Typeface... Go on it's FUN....

Font Name: _____
Date: _____
Designer: _____

Aa   Bb   Cc   Dd   Ee   Ff   Gg

Hh   Ii   Jj   Kk   Ll   Mm   Nn   Oo   Pp

Qq   Rr   Ss   Tt   Uu   Vv   Ww   Xx   Yy   Zz

CHAPTER TWO

TAKE A DEEP BREATH, HOLD UP YOUR
PENCIL AND REPEAT AFTER ME:

I CAN DRAW!
I CAN DRAW!
I CAN DRAW!

NOW ROAR LIKE A SPARTAN KING.

Drawing is FUN because Drawing is FUN!
AND FUN IS DRAWING!

If Writing is BROCCOLI then drawing is CAKE.

They call you the ~~doodle~~ DANCER!

NOBODY shows other people their sentences like:
"Hey Buddy check out this sentence I wrote-Woah! Cool."
People are all like showing each other their drawings
though, right?
This is because...

COOL PEOPLE DO DRAWINGS

THE BLANK PAGE IS _NO_ THREAT to YOU. YOU ARE the MAKER OF MARKS, THE DrEAMER OF PEN BASED DREAMS.

MYSELF PORTRAIT

START WITH
YOUR OWN
F A C E!!
ADD A PAIR OF
GREAT EYES,
WILD HAIR....

FIND A PHOTOGRAPH & PASTE IT HERE

OR THERE

NOW get a SET OF COLOURED PENS AND CREATE SOMETHING WONDERFUL WITH IT!

DRAW SOMETHING REALLY QUICKLY!

DRAW SOMETHING REALLY SLOOOOWLY

DRAW YOUR OWN TATTOO!

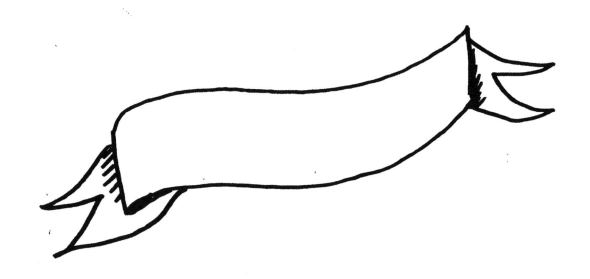

"DRAW THE PALM OF YOUR HAND

LISTEN TO A SONG AND DRAW
SOME DOODLES INSPIRED BY THE MUSIC:

LALAALA

Name of the Song: _____

DIA de LOS MUERTOS

DESIGN AND COLOUR IN YOUR OWN MEXICAN 'DAY OF THE DEAD' SUGAR SKULL!

"DESIGN YOUR OWN" SNEAKERS

LIMITED EDITION, BOX FRESH!

These sneakers are so fly I cannot even put my feet upon the earth. I have to wear them inside a specially constructed vacuum so that no spec of dust may land upon them!

BE HOLD!

Draw your FRIENDS & FAMILY

There is a new technology in town that will soon make cameras a thing of the past.
It's called DOING A DRAWING OF A FACE. It'll be the new selfie...

GET on BOARD NOW!
before it blows!

GRAB a PENCIL CLOSE YOUR EYESSS

Grab a pencil, close your eyes and just start
drawing. Keep your tiny eyes closed.
Keep your pen on the paperat all times.Think
about anything you like and draw it. Remember
eyes closed, pen on paper, fill the page and VOILA!

POSTER

Remember, we live in the real world.
WHAT DID YOU Do TODAY????
CREATE a poster that shouts to the world what
you have done today!

POWER

POWER OF the COLLAGE

I. Get hold of a magazine.
2. Find images of peoples heads
3. Stick them onto the opposite page
4. Now, cut out noses,mouths, eyes, arms ,legs or
   whatever you want and stick it onto the faces.
5. MIX IT UP.
6. GO FOR IT!

EVERY THING ON THIS PAGE IS JUST AN IDEA. YOU CAN USE YOUR OWN!

EYE

EYE

NOSE

USE SCISSORS & GLUE FOR THAT COLLAGE. AND YOUR IMAGINATION!

ARMS, LEGS BIG FEET

LEFT ARM OR LEG OR...

MOUTH

ADD DOODLES TO MAKE IT BETTER!

ADD SOMETHING HILARIOUS HERE.

THIS COULD BE WHATEVER YOU THINK IT'S FUNNY! ANIMAL PARTS, CARWHEELS...

MAKE your OWN MASK

Masks

A mask creates a barrier of make-believe between yourself and the rest of the world. You can hide behind it. No one will know who you are. You simply disappear, since most people recognise you only by your face. This is the reason why many people throughout the world believe that there is magic in wearing a mask. By putting one on you actually become whatever it represents – another person, animal or spirit. While wearing it you can achieve things you could not ordinarily do.

YEAH! OK! LET'S JUST DO THIS NOW!
FINISH THE MASKS! USE THEM AS inspiration and MAKE YOUR OWN ONES! GET WILD! ROOARRR!!

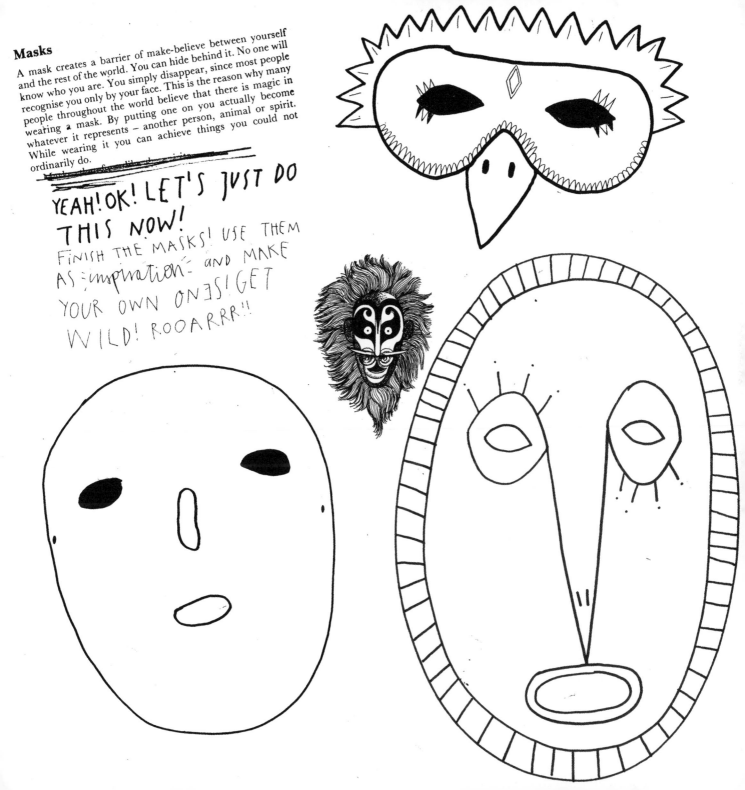

CREATE your OWN COMIC STRIP!

Marvel at your own genius. Write about a magical world, superhero, supervillian or talking animal. Make it slapstick, graphic novel or cartoon. YOU CHOOSE. Create stick figures like a Grade A UNDER ACHIEVER. Go on DO A COMIC!!!!

Start by sketching your ideas down on a separate piece of paper so you know what's going to happen in each panel. CREATE CHARACTERS & SCENES and don't forget the dialogue & ACTION. MIX IT UP ! And don't forget your story needs a beginning a middle and an end. Or does it.....???

LIST OF MAIN CHARACTERS + SKETCHES:

NAME: _____

NAME: _____

NAME: _____

TITLE & NAME & LOGO OF YOUR COMIC:

LOGO:

NAME: _____

THE ADVENTURE BEGINS ⟶

MEANWHILE IN....

WHEN THE GOON hits your FLY LIKE a STUFFED PIZZA pie THAT'2 AMORE

It's your turn CHEF.

Put all your favourite toppings
on this very special PIZZA.

Then give it a name and try to order it!

NAME: _____

TOPPINGS: _____

Mmm.....

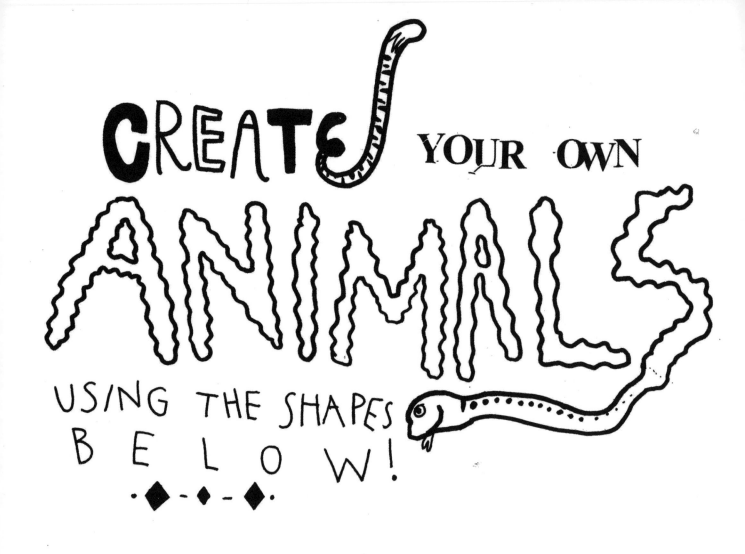

CREATE YOUR OWN ANIMALS USING THE SHAPES BELOW!

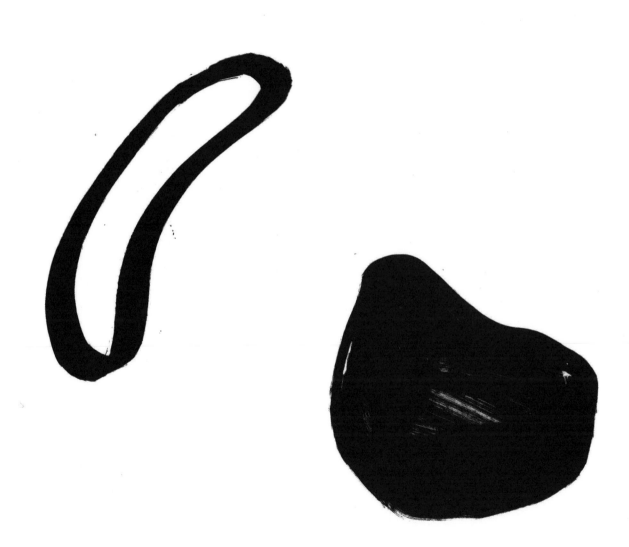

CREATE your CLAN

CLANS ARE TYPICALLY JUST GROUPS OF PEOPLE WITH COMMON INTERESTS. THAT COULD ~~BE~~ MEAN, SPORTS, HOBBIES, PIZZA OR GROUPS WITH SIMILAR PASSIONS.

Generate your _own_ clan name by choosing one of the words from each side! (or you can make your own!!)

		PICK ONE!	
WOODEN			CATS
RED			BANANAS
NINJA			KINGS
RIDERS OF			LIFE
BIG			GIRLS
RANDOM	←	→	BOYS
VAMPIRE			LIONS
TEARS OF			CREW
TWISTED			UNIT
SILVER			UNICORNS
FAST	←	→	FUN
KINGS OF			TEAM

YOUR CLAN:

TEAM NAME: _____

LEADERS NAME: _____

CLAN TAG: _____

CLAN MEMBERS: _____

_____

CLAN LOGO:

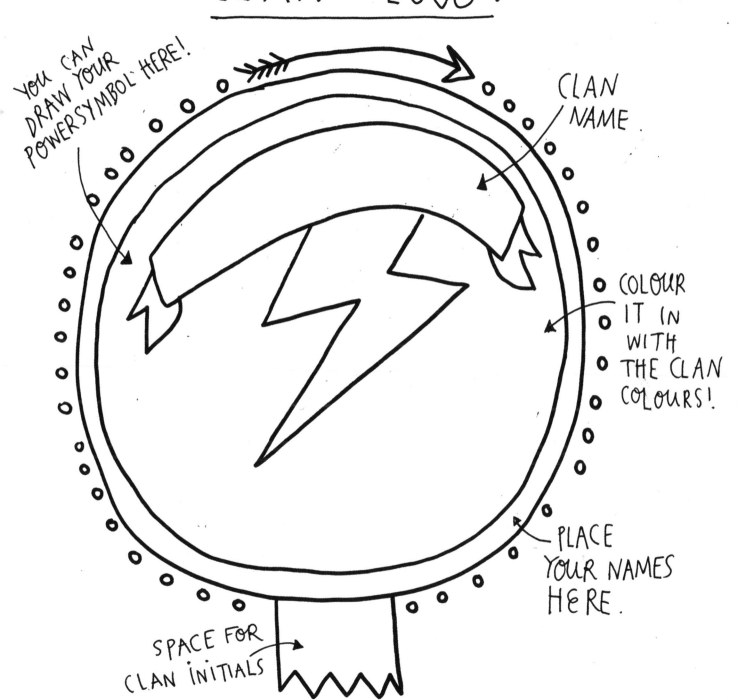

YOU CAN DRAW YOUR POWERSYMBOL HERE!

CLAN NAME

COLOUR IT IN WITH THE CLAN COLOURS!

PLACE YOUR NAMES HERE.

SPACE FOR CLAN INITIALS

DOODLE 'n GO

Make these photographs more fun!
YOU can do this, I show you a little bit but then it's
on you. GO FOR IT. PIMP MY PIC, ...

Add speechbubbles, mustaches, eyes, patterns ,colour....

BRAIN

DESIGN YOUR OWN T-SHIRT

WRITE YOUR NAME in the following STYLES:

BUBBLE

Shadow:

MY LIFE IN NUMBERS

10 THINGS I LOVE:

8 Things I want to do:

9 THINGS THAT BORE ME:

7 THINGS I'M GOOD AT

6 THINGS I LIKE TO EAT

5 things that make ME HAPPY

4 THINGS I'M REALLY BAD AT

3 things I have LOST...

2 THINGS I HAVE FOUND:

1 thing that I like to DO:

LUCHA THIS!

Lucha Libre is a legendary type of professional wrestling from Mexico. that translates as 'FREE FIGHT'.

Its SUPERHERO wrestlers are characterized by crazy colourful masks depicting animals, gods and ancient heroes & they fight using a combination of fast moves and acrobatic high flying dives.

IMAGINE YOU ARE A LUCHADORE or a LUCHADORAI !!!

SO WHAT IS YOUR MEXICAN WRESTLING NAME?

el tornado fantastico   -LA COBRA-   EL BURRITO

El Dorito
EL PARASOL

MY NAME:

what is your special move:

What's your catchphrase:

What are your fighting colours:

Why are you so feared in the ring:

NOW CREATE `YOUR` `OWN` LUCHA LIBRE MASK!

MAYBE PATTERNS!

YOU CAN USE THIS SHAPE, OR IGNORE IT A MAKE YOUR OWN!

OFTEN A BIT OF GLITTER HELPS!

USE BRIGHT COLOURS!

COLOUR THE BACKGROUND IN TOO!

VIVA LA LUCHA LIBRE

CHAPTER
THREE

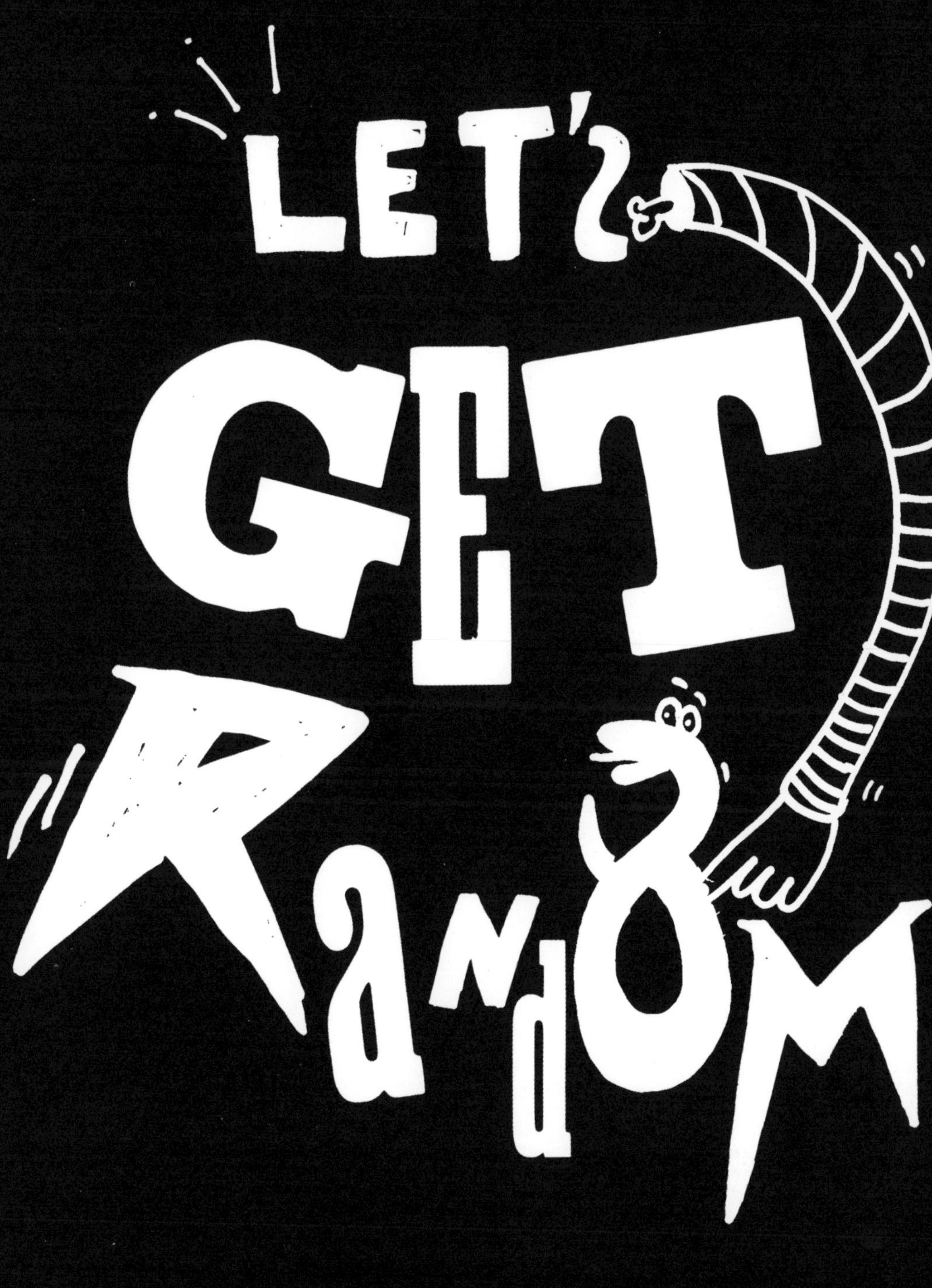
LET'S GET RANDOM

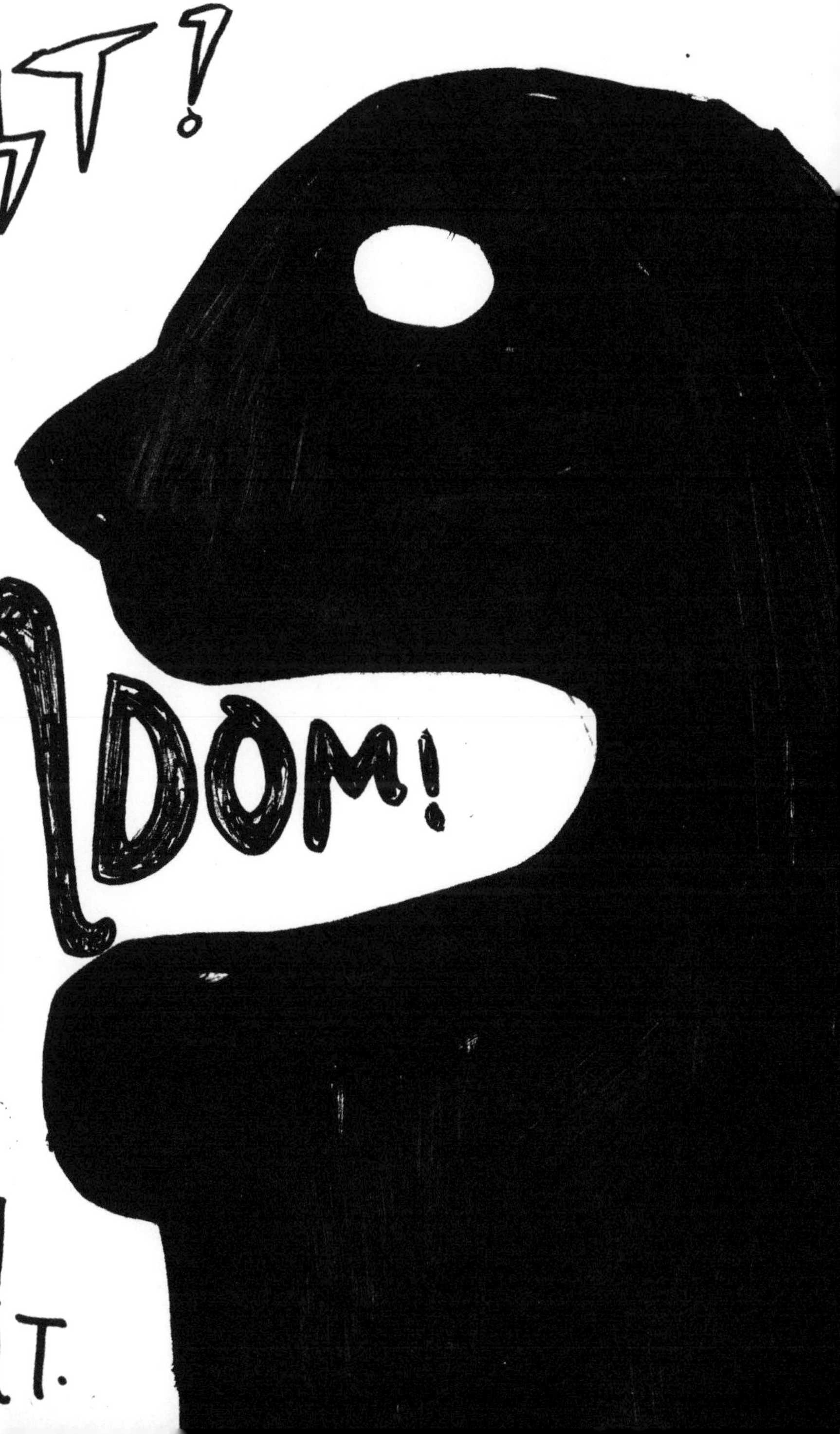

WHAT'S YOUR DEFINITION OF RANDOM? IF IT'S NOT THE SAME AS THE one IN THE DICTIONARY, CHANCES ARE YOU ARE SIMPLY WRONG!

A RANDOM DOG.

NAME: _____

AGE: _____

  COLOUR: _____ ____

SIZE: _____

RANDOM:
Unexpected(unless you were expecting
the unexpected in which case only the
expected would be unexpected & therefore
it would be also expected.)

PLEASE STOP READING THIS
WE'RE BOTH TRAPPED
HERE UNTIL YOU DO SOMETHING
RANDOM

WRITE A LETTER
.... EXPLAINING WHY YOUR PARENTS HAVE TO TAKE YOU TO A THEME PARK!!

DEAR.

MUM & DAD

I CAN'T DANCE !!
THAT'S even better!

PRACTICE A LITTLE DANCE ROUTINE AND THEN
START DANCING AT ANY RANDOM TIME!
Before breakfast, in the Shops, at the BUS STOP...

NOTES ON MY DANCE:

_____
_____
_____
_____
_____
_____
_____ DO THE DANCE!

SONG I LIKE TO DANCE TO: _____

POWER UP: FOR SOME EXTRA RANDOM CREDIBILITY
INVOLVE FAMILY, FRIENDS & PETS!

HOW MANY TIMES CAN YOU
CLAP BETWEEN THROWING A
BALL IN THE AIR AND CATCHING IT ?

ANSWER: _____

CAN YOU WALK AROUND THE LIVING
ROOM ≡WITHOUT≡ TOUCHING THE FLOOR?
☐ YES   ☐ NO

CAN YOU WIGGLE YOUR EARS?
☐ YES ☐ NO ☐ potato

CAN YOU LICK YOUR EAR?
☐ YES   ☐ NO

CAN YOU TOUCH YOUR **NOSE**
WITH YOUR *tongue?*

ANSWER: _____

LEARN A JOKE...

hahaha!

...And memorize it!!! WHENEVER YOU MEET NEW PEOPLE TRY TO SLIP IT INTO CONVERSATION, BINGO!!!

WHAT DO YOU CALL CHEESE THAT ISN'T YOURS? NACHO CHEESE!

YOU'RE A BONE FIDE COMEDIAN

WHY DID THE COOKIE GO TO THE HOSPITAL →He felt CRUMMY!

TAKE A BLANK
PAGE & GIVE IT
TO YOUR MUM.

TELL HER IT IS YOUR
BEST DRAWING

OPEN THE DICTIONARY AND LEARN
3 NEW WORDS. TRY TO GET
THEM INTO CONVERSATION
WITH THE NEXT PERSON
YOU MEET.

LEARN A MAGIC TRICK.
WHEN YOU MEET NEW PEOPLE...
...AMAZE THEM WITH YOUR
MAGIC SKILLS!

WRITE THE MOST WEIRD, RANDOM, CRAZY SENTENCE YOU CAN THINK OF THEN TEXT IT TO SOMEONE YOU KNOW WITHOUT ANY EXPLANATIONS. (REFUSE TO EXPLAIN IT!)

Draw a picture of your house with your eyes closed!

RANDOM Remix

Yeah, yeah, yeah nature is pretty cool...   BUT WE CAN DO BETTER.
Use the following random combinations of words and make
your own drawings by creating crazy objects and creatures
YOU LIKE IT?

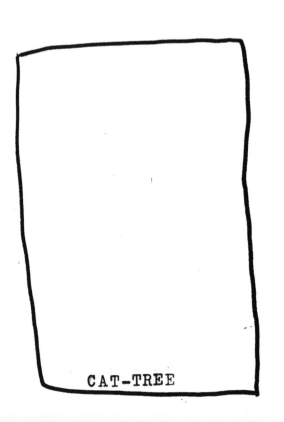

CAT-TREE

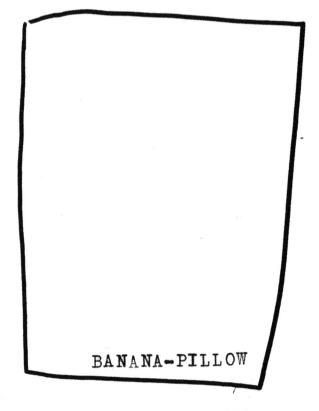

BANANA-PILLOW

SUPER SOFT!

NOSE-BRUSH

BOTTLE-PANTS

PHONE-BALL

SHOE-PLANE

WORM-WARMER

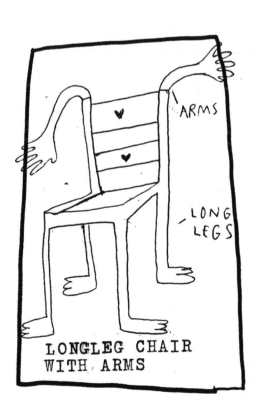

ARMS

LONG LEGS

LONGLEG CHAIR
WITH ARMS

CHAPTER
FOUR

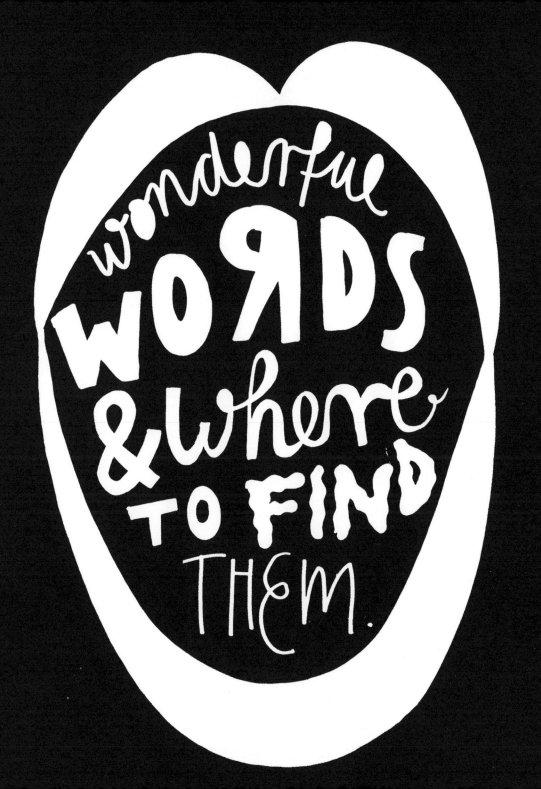

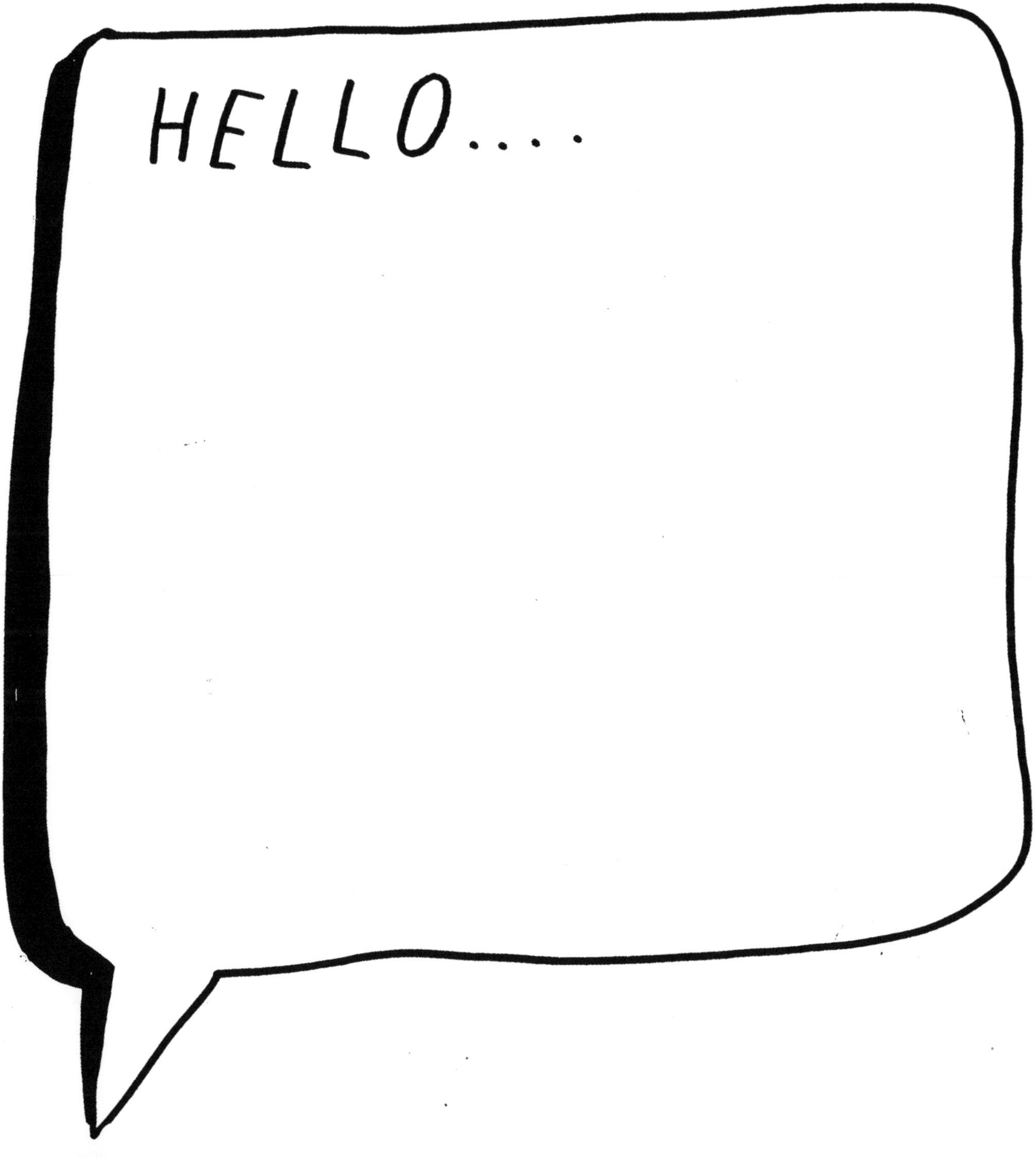
HELLO....

SPEND THE NIGHT IN A GRAVEYARD — SPEND THE NIGHT IN AN ABANDONED HOUSE

JUMP OUT OF A PLANE — DO A BUNGEE JUMP

HAVE A PET CROCODILE — HAVE A PET TIGER

SLEEP ON A BED OF NAILS — WALK ON HOT COALS

GO BACK IN TIME — GO FORWARD IN TIME

HAVE X-RAY VISION — BIONIC HEARING

ONE WISH TODAY — THREE WISHES IN TEN YEARS TIME

HAVE EXTRA LONG LEGS — HAVE A LONG NECK

BE ABLE TO TALK TO ANIMALS — BE FLUENT IN EVERY LANGUAGE

BE ABLE TO READ MINDS — BE ABLE TO BE INVISIBLE

BE ABLE TO JUMP SUPER HIGH — BE ABLE TO RUN SUPER FAST

OWN A CHOCOLATE FACTORY — OWN A ICE CREAM FACTORY

WORD POWER

HERE ARE SOME NEW WORDS TO POWER UP YOUR VOCABULARY!

Brouhaha → An uproar

Vomitory → Exit

GONGOOZLE → To stare at

Eructation → Burp

DISCOMBOBULATED → To confuse

SHENANIGAN → prank

NOW TRY AND GET YOUR NEW WORDS INTO CONVERSATION THROUGHOUT THE DAY!

HERE'S SOME EXAMPLES: "MUM, that person on the other side of the road is gongoozlin me."

"we had maths today, I got really discombobulated."

Should we leave through the side vomitory?

ALWAYS BE → PREPARED

IT MIGHT BE GOOD TO HAVE SOME
OF THE FOLLOWING STATEMENTS, POEMS
QUESTIONS AND LETTERS READY IN YOUR
BACK POCKET.... you never know!

1. WRITE A LOVE POEM.

2. WRITE A LOVE LETTER TO YOUR PET.

3. WHAT QUESTIONS WOULD YOU ASK YOUR FAVOURITE CELEBRITY.

ASK ME
ASK ME
ASK ME

Life is better when you ask more questions.
You'll soon discover that your family and friends
are very interesting ...
HOW IS THAT SO?

Well, because everyone is fascinating in their own way.

Go get someone you know (parent, sister,brother,
aunt,uncle,cat, dog, budgie) and both of you grab
a seat onthe sofa and make yourself comfy. Use the
questions on the opposite page to conduct a mini interview,
when you come across a question that interests you try
to find out more about what they really think.

Just what have they got to say?
Its just like an interview with a celebrity.

NOW IT'S YOUR TURN.
GET THEM TO SWITCH SIDES AND INTERVIEW YOU TOO.

Do you wish you were famous?

What's your favourite thing to do?

Tell me something that you don't like?

What is your favourite movie of all time?

Who is the most famous person you have met?

Would you rather have 2000 instagram followers or 2 good friends?

What's your favourite ice cream flavour?

What was your favourite subject at school?

What's the biggest thing on your mind right now?

What is your current favourite programme on TV?

Growing up, who inspired you the most?

Are we alone in the universe?

If you had a boat what would you name it?

If you could drive any car what would it be?

What's your favourite book?

What could you not live without?

How much toast is too much?

What's your favourite food?

Blaaa... bla bla...

Go AND INTERVIEW SOMEONE.

If you started running right now how far could you go without stopping?

What is your favourite cheese?

If you could have a walk on part in any movie what would you choose?

What would you do if you won ten million on the lottery?

What is your favourite snack?

If you could go anywhere in the world on holiday right now where would you go?

How much money is enough?

and finally . . .

If you could go back and give your 10-year-old self one piece of advice what would it be?

ONCE UPON A TIME...

Write your own Fantasy Story, knights, pirates, unicorns, dragons, wild creatures and crazy locations, everything is allowed...

Just make sure it has a happy ending....

TO THE FUTURE and Beyond

IMAGINATION STARTS right HERE! and has no LIMITS

IMAGINE YOU ARE GOING ON AN EXPLORATION TO TRACK
DOWN THE LOST GOLD OF THE INCAS....

WHAT WOULD
YOU TAKE
WITH YOU?

WHO

NAME:

would you take with you?

HOW WOULD YOU GET THERE?

COMBINE YOUR SKILLS CREATE YOUR FUTURE

Draw yourself ten years from now.

Sketch the city of the future.

Draw the car of the future.

SAVING FOR YOUR FUTURE ADVENTURES

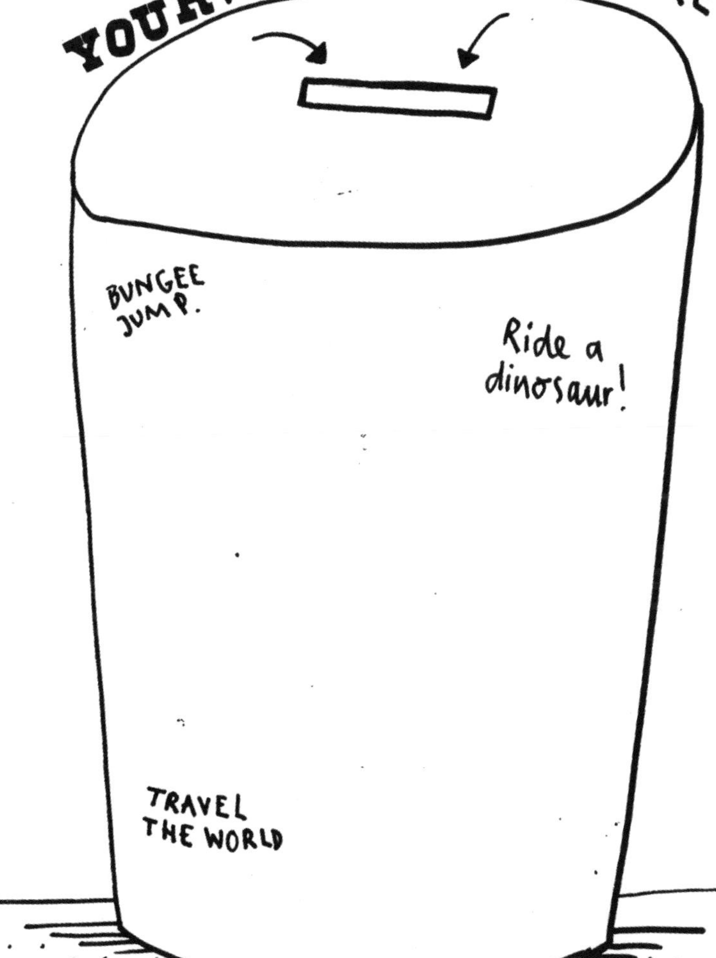

write down all the adventures you want to do in the future!

WE ARE IN THE YEAR 2050½.
PEOPLE travel to

MARS!

CAN YOU DRAW THE FIRST

ALIEN

SEEN THERE?

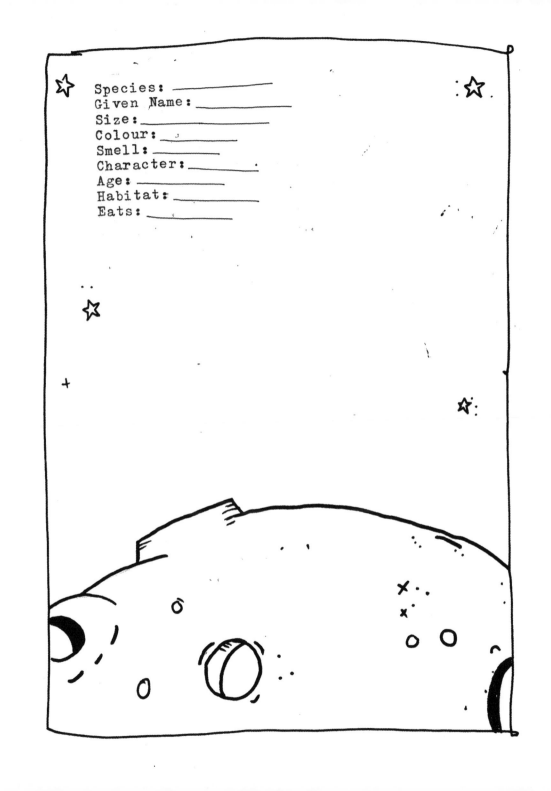

Species: _____
Given Name: _____
Size: _____
Colour: _____
Smell: _____
Character: _____
Age: _____
Habitat: _____
Eats: _____

Monster MASH

WILD

FUTURE FUTURE FUTURE! !

No one knows what the future will
bring... well YOU DO.
New creatures on planet earth...
Draw your own little future monsters..
They can be fluffy, soft or hard and heavy
it's up to you. Don't forget to name the
little guys.

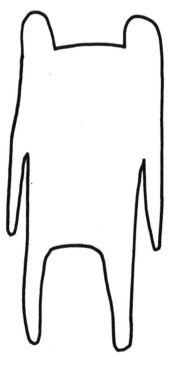

I WISH
I WISH...

In this game you cannot wish for infinite wishes
because a genie will come and steal your fingers
and replace them with chocolate fingers.
We won't accept any responsibility for this.

I WOULD LIKE TO LEARN _____

I WOULD LIKE TO TRAVEL TO _____

I WISH I COULD SEE _____

I WISH I DIDN'T HAVE TO EAT _____

I WISH I COULD ALWAYS EAT _____

I WISH I HAD A MILLION _____

~~I WISH I HAD~~

I WISH I HAD A _____

I WISH I DIDN'T HAVE TO _____

I WISH I COULD _____

I WISH I COULD SAVE _____

~~I WISH I~~

the BUCKET List...

So what are the things you absolutely need to do? Tick them off this list & start your own.

- ☑ SNOWBOARD
- ☐ CANOE
- ☐ RIDE A CAMEL
- ☐ PLAY A MUSICAL INSTRUMENT
- ☐ LEARN A DANCE
- ☐ VISIT LONDON
- ☐ SKYDIVE
- ☐ SCUBA DIVE
- ☐ DIVE WITH SHARKS
- ☐ MAKE POTTERY
- ☐ WRITE A SHORT STORY
- ☐ WRITE A BOOK
- ☐ CLIMB A MOUNTAIN
- ☐ PLANT A TREE
- ☐ FLY IN A HELICOPTER

- ☐ VISIT PARIS
- ☐ GO HIKING
- ☐ GIVE TO CHARITY
- ☐ GO ROCK CLIMBING
- ☐ LEARN TO JUGGLE
- ☐ LEARN TO KNIT
- ☐ MAKE A MUSIC VIDEO
- ☐ BREAK A WORLD RECORD
- ☐ STROKE A LION
- ☐ FLY TO THE MOON
- ☐ SEE A SHOOTING STAR
- ☐ SEE AN ECLIPSE
- ☐ VISIT THE NORTHPOLE
- ☐ RIDE A HORSE
- ☐ VISIT NEW YORK
- ☐ MAKE YOUR OWN PIZZA

- ☐ _____
- ☐ _____
- ☐ _____
- ☐ _____
- ☐ _____
- ☐ _____
- ☐ _____
- ☐ _____
- ☐ _____
- ☐ _____
- ☐ _____
- ☐ _____
- ☐ _____

UNITED STATES of ADVENTURE LAND

HELLO MR./MRS. PRESIDENT.

Wow you made it. You are president.
What would you change first? What are the ten
new rules and laws for your great country?

1. _____

2. _____

3. _____

4. _____

5. _____

6. _____

7. _____

8. _____

9. _____

10. _____

BEST
PRESIDENT
EVER

CHAPTER
SIX

The END is just the BEGINNING

DONE

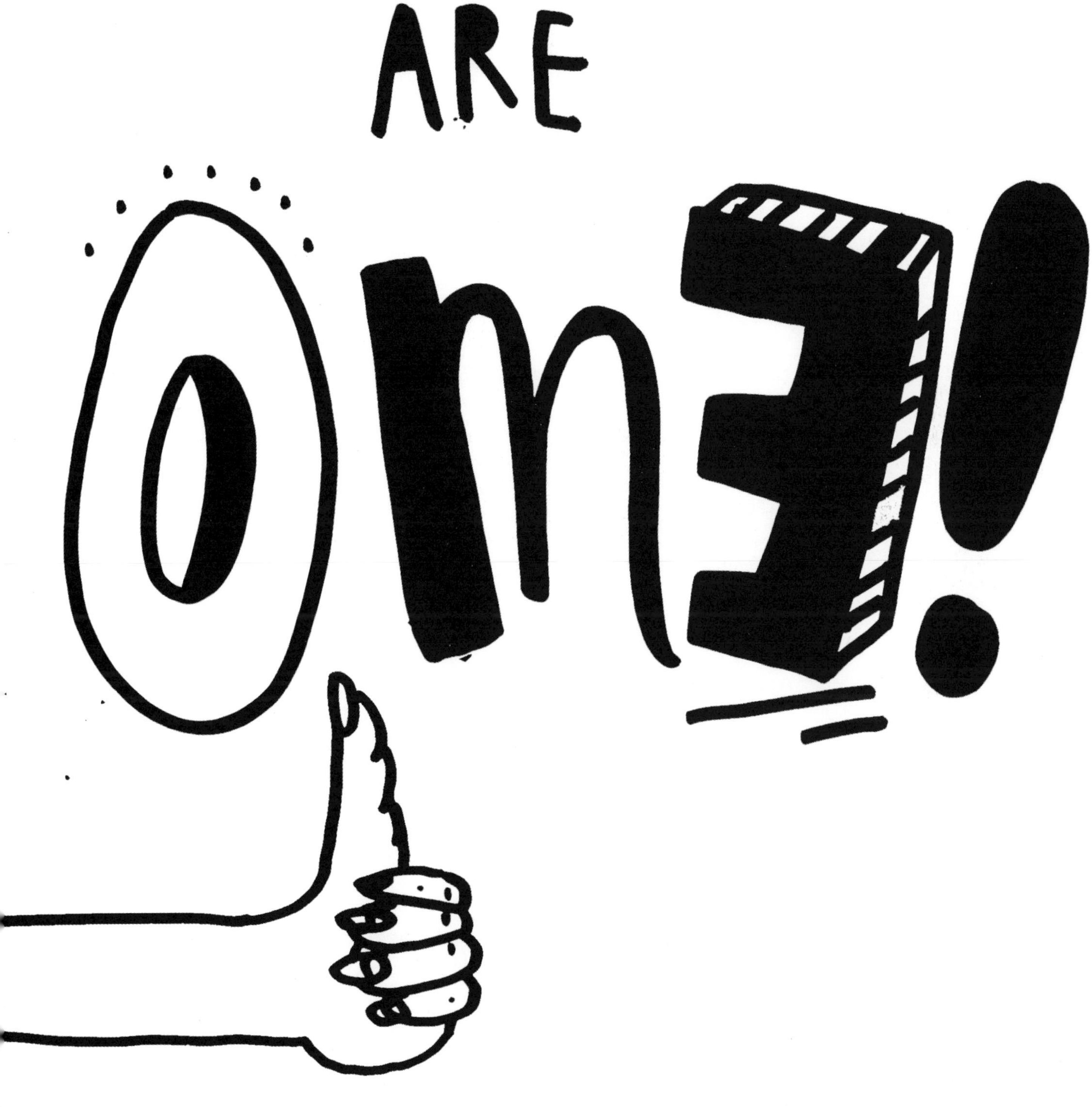
ARE
OME!

YOU HAVE NOW LEARNED A LOT ABOUT DRAWING, seeing, hearing, WRITING, OBSERVING, ANALYZING, SNAKES, MAGIC TRICKS, WIZARDS, music, THE FUTURE, THE PAST, PIZZA, POETRY, NVTURE, dancing, THE GALAXY, PORTRAITS, PEOPLE & MANY MANY more....

BUT (t)

THE MOST IMPORTANT THING IS THAT YOU'VE LEARNED A LOT ABOUT YOURSELF AND WHAT YOU CAN CREATE AND HOW MUCH FUN IT IS.

THE TIME CAPSULE

The Time Capsule Guidelines

By the time you have finished this book it should be almost like a living thing. IT's so full of your crazy brain magic it will practically throb. Good. Now is the time for the final mission.

It's best to do this in the light of the moon.

Wrap the book up in loads of clingfilm. Now wrap it up again in bits of wrapping paper or whatever you can find. Put it inside ten bags one after the other. Wrap it up in loads of sellotape. Stuff in in a box or a tin.

Now find a hiding place, maybe bury it in the garden or whatever you can think of. Put a message on it saying:

        TIME CAPSULE) - DO NOT OPEN UNTIL .... ↰
                      (put a year on thirteen years from now)

Say some magic words.

The world turns.

AFK....BRB!

Do not return for 13 years.